May and Marta and Max

by Marilee Robin Burton

illustrated by Amy Wummer

Scott Foresman

Editorial Offices: Glenview, Illinois • New York, New York
Sales Offices: Reading, Massachusetts • Duluth, Georgia
Glenview, Illinois • Carrollton, Texas • Menlo Park, California

Last week I had a best friend.

May was my best friend. We did
everything together. We sang. We
danced. We made up stories. May
was my very best friend!

We even had our own club. We
called it the May and Marta Club.

Max Hill wanted to be in
our club. But we said, "No!"

Max Hill could not be in the May and Marta Club. That would not make any sense! Besides, May and Marta makes two . . . the perfect number.

But that was last week. Last week my
best friend was May. Last week May
and I were in a club. Last week May and
I did everything together.

This week is not the same. This week May is home. This week May is sick. This week I am the only one in the May and Marta Club. And that does not make sense.

So, I thought about Max Hill.
Maybe he could be in the May
and Marta Club . . . but just for
a few days.

I went up to Max at lunch. I said,
"Do you want to be in the May and
Marta Club . . . just for a few days?"

Max took a sip of his milk. He
said, "Okay. Sure."

Max is not the same as May.
He doesn't sing. He doesn't dance.
He doesn't make up stories.

Max is not the same as May.
Max tells jokes! Max climbs trees!
Max juggles!

Max said, "Let's put on a show for May. It will make her feel better."

I thought about May. She must be lonely. It's not fun to be all alone.

So Max and I put together a show.
I sang. I danced. Max juggled a few ice
cubes. Max told jokes. Max was fun!

Max said, "Let's call it the Max and
Marta Show."

And I said, "Okay, sure."

We put on our show in May's yard.
She watched from inside. Now I'm
not sure if the show did the trick. But
it was a good show! The very next
day May was well.

Last week I had a best friend. We were in the May and Marta Club. But that was then and this is now. Now I have two best friends. Three is a very good number. And we are in the May, Marta, and Max Club.